AF148825

About the Author

In 1977, Anil Agrawal got his post graduation degree in Modern History at the University of Allahabad. Since childhood, he took a keen interest in creative writing. His mental ailment of Schizophrenia has its traces in him being oversensitive. Researches confirm what psychologists say that people with higher sensitivity are good performers. Moreover, as our society gets more automated, the need for people with intuition, creativity and empathy becomes even greater. And it is for sure that the abilities of sensitive people cannot be reproduced by technology.

Presently he is editing a bilingual monthly magazine on current affairs for civil services aspirants here in India. His son is a former civil judge, and his spouse is a former educator.

Life Lessons (A Schizophrenian File)

Anil Agrawal

Life Lessons (A Schizophrenian File)

Olympia Publishers
London

www.olympiapublishers.com
OLYMPIA PAPERBACK EDITION

Copyright © Anil Agrawal 2023

The right of Anil Agrawal to be identified as author of
this work has been asserted in accordance with sections 77 and 78 of
the Copyright, Designs and Patents Act 1988.

All Rights Reserved

No reproduction, copy or transmission of this publication
may be made without written permission.
No paragraph of this publication may be reproduced,
copied or transmitted save with the written permission of the publisher,
or in accordance with the provisions
of the Copyright Act 1956 (as amended).

Any person who commits any unauthorised act in relation to
this publication may be liable to criminal
prosecution and civil claims for damage.

A CIP catalogue record for this title is
available from the British Library.

ISBN: 978-1-80074-962-7

This is a work of fiction.
Names, characters, places and incidents originate from the writer's
imagination. Any resemblance to actual persons, living or dead, is
purely coincidental.

First Published in 2023

Olympia Publishers
Tallis House
2 Tallis Street
London
EC4Y 0AB

Printed in Great Britain

Dedication

I dedicate this book to my father the late Dr Ishwar Nath Agrawal, former professor at the University of Allahabad, Allahabad.

Acknowledgements

I do humbly acknowledge the pains that my wife, Neelam Agrawal, took in getting things right in a presentable format.

LIFE

Unless you suffer in life, you will miss the content of a
meaningful life
Life is always unjust to those
Who are just unto themselves
Life is!
How you take and feel it
Nothing more, nothing less
Your instinct to put questions across
Is the single most pertinent answer of your vibes of self-
betterment
You don't have to be perfect to achieve something better or
great
Being ordinary, being natural, will bring great accolades
Don't lose people who matter
Because your recognition will be in jeopardy?
Life is fearful
For its uncertain rhythm
Wherever the disintegration of family is taking place in the
world
Man's loneliness has increased tenfold
Family basically is a cocoon
Family used to be a shelter for Unfortunates in a family
With its disintegration
The Unfortunates of a family have taken to the streets
Always settle for less

Or you tax your mind
Run with the clock
You will reach early
When you are at crossroads with your inner self
You cannot manifest anything
Become passionate
And be triumphant
Don't just decry conformity
It has History behind it!
Time circuses a thin ropeway
Never belittle anyone
Every man is thrown flattened once, twice or thrice by life
Your arising is what matters
We are not possessive of what we get
And tend to push things into memories
And then become nostalgic
Rigid is not adaptable
Flexibility is! What do you choose?
Our survival instinct is intertwined with adaptability
Choosing your path
And your choices
Are the two worthwhile submissions
Which a man ought to follow
Life is one asset
That cannot be reclaimed
One's choosing to live in gratitude
Shouldn't be an investment
Rather a pious duty
If your shadow chases you
You are running towards the furnace
Never make it happen that your shadow chases you

Going to simply growing
Simply keep going
One who loses the gamble
Has a green signal for winning it too
You can change the beginning?
Just by making it less virtuous than the end!
We are living in this nascent century where
The fulcrum of man's perspective is getting blurred
In this age we are losing our capacity
To understand things
In a healthy perspective!
A sickening predicament
To know is enough in itself
If you want disquiet
Go for understanding
Don't go for defeating darkness
Pray for an early dawn
Life is simply very gratifying
It gives man very many chances
To improve, create and manifest
All you have to do is
To live purposefully
Fixing anyone or situation
Never solves the issue
Life isn't meant for holding anything
It's for letting go of everything
To do good things to others, always
Is the only Definition of life
Sublimity must accompany
Only by going through life, one grows!
Is there any other way to grow?
Pushing oneself forward is the essence of life

As far as the meaning of life is concerned
The scriptures, dogmas and religion only tell about
duties to be performed in life
What is life they never tell?
Life is an occasion given to a chosen one
To relish this forceful nature
To love, to be loved, to be loving
And to partner procreation
Thereby giving an unending chain of happenings…
You cannot have everything in life
You wish
Life's purpose has no consensus
As many people, as many meanings
Life has more lessons, some of them hilarious
Than in a hundred books
In life there are two rights
And definitively two wrongs
Too
You get in life what you are ordained to…
World is nothing more than an onlooker
A win is the thinnest happening
People are misers in giving their appreciation
They just gulp
Enjoy the journey
Arriving is finishing
Too much learning is a curse
For a better living we should unlearn many a thing
Ignorance, in some way is a bliss, in many situations
Certainty propels
Colour conditions behaviour
There are phases in life when you cannot achieve

Anything
Whether you pour your mind or sweat
It's God's way
Opening and closing of doors is an obsolete happening
Now email jumps into your bedroom
We all have a phase of bad days in our lives
In a study a man with seventy years life span will go through
A minimum of twenty years lean period
This you can very well assume a law unto itself
The quality of our life much depends on our successfully
Implementing the minimal lifestyle agenda
Colour of the skin nowadays decides destiny
Attitude is attitudinal
Its leverage is huge.

SCHIZOPHRENIA

Suicide needs no meddling
It has been there, since and it will be there
People who take to suicide
Are passionate souls
A man who undervalues himself
Is sure to be a victim of depression
Mental illness is tiptoed
It just grabs
If you are scared of something that doesn't exist
It is sure that you suffer from some mental ailment
For bipolar people
Hope is their first causality
They are just helpless!
Always live with your insanity
Believe in your waywardness
You become great?
In your bipolar world
You just can't face anyone
Even yourself!
In any mental illness
Your only ally is your destiny
People leave one by one
Until you start roaming in streets
Alone!
Unless you attain a certain level of insanity

You can't manifest
Great achievers were insane people
Less sleep would lead to constipation
A much visible mental logjam
In bipolarity mind overarches
Heart palpitates fast
And skin is red faced
And your gut health simmers
Just don't be too touchy and sensitive
Or you will reap Schizophrenia
Schizophrenia makes your in-laws your adversaries
For they become too possessive of their siblings
If you want to be an optimist
Make the moon your idol
It will take care of your mood-swings
My optimism
Or pessimism
Surfaced
Only when I was destined for!
Mood-swings are invariably governed
By the placement of the Moon in any horoscope
It is a proven fact for years on and!
This is what it feels like
Misery rotates I have had my turn
One should always be prepared for
Their opportunity
Love deprivation drives one mental
It stunts growth
Love should be free
Non-negotiable, untagged
I am not a bachelor

Yet I am to manifest a kiss
One of the many reasons that
Drove me mental
Mothers are always poised for a great
Relationship with their siblings
Her love-hate see-saw with her dear ones
Goes many a time in making the child suffer
From psychological abuse
Mothers are primordial reasons
For their child's personality
Fissures
If you are a mental patient
It is not because your
Mind is diseased
Just so
Because your moon
Sign is dilapidated
My illness taught...
Faith always puts you
In perspective
Where you want
Yourself seeing
My faith in God
Made me bounce back
From the messy schizophrenia
Over thinking is a sickening mental vibe
It unsettles
Too much and too
Loud of it
Makes you timid
I never prayed for a Heal

Time, I have!
Is the greatest
Healer
With time
We Heal
If you can bend all around
And all about
You become mentally
Partaking
The unexpected
Is always in time
With your destiny!
Being happy amidst pain is the
Shortest way to success
Those who dare to thrive in pain and agony
Create success stories
The story of my life
Was wept away
Still I staged a comeback
Every pain has a
Stakeholder of
Pleasure too
For one's betterment
One has to claim oneself!
To pre-empt any mental logjam
Child behaviour must always
Be given push-ups
During my ill days
People taught me that
Work will go without
Even you
People with mental illness

Don't even get the benefit of
Sympathy...
A commonplace
Human vibe
I can and I will
Was never the
Phraseology in the nineties
Still, I emulated it
Then
The challenge of
Life is to overcome it
The essence to take care of
Oneself
Physiological abuses during
Childhood are the failings of most
Upbringings
Schizophrenia is your obsession with
Yourself to a maddening extent
A mental patient is never
Cajoled into love
Love never gushes for a mental
A convenient distance keeps
Things down the line
I, many a times was begging for love.

HEART

The question is
Is the heart really intelligent?
Not really
Its staple is impulse
How else we see often, a Beauty chasing a Beast?
For creating a work that has deep impact
You have to pour your heart and soul.
Not mind but heart is our great warrior
Battles are won by heart alone
Instead of your pocket
Make your heart rich
Heart, not mind is your soulmate
It is the pathfinder to your journey
The best version of yourself
Is always aligned to your palpable heart
Don't optimize your brain
Enlarge your heart
The art of healing
Emanates from your heart
Brain is a blocker
There is a universe to explore not inside your head
But your heart
Eyes reflect your heart
Heart speaks
The language of deaf and dumb

If you have a pure heart
You start striking the right chord all around
If you behave by your heart
You will definitively achieve anything
A kind man at heart
Is befooled again and again
He just can't change his sensuous heart
A clean heart is always better than a good heart
The most wonderful place to be in the world is
In the inner recesses of your heart
Where Almighty's Blissful showers of benevolences are
Your heart and soul are always on fire
They need your inklings to manifest
The heart cannot see
It just senses and smells
The vibes that push it up
Believe your heart
Even it is blind!
Heart is never there for determination
Your mind may well determine
Heartbeat is your life rhythm

ALMIGHTY

Sun is the only visible God
We can choose our beginning
But, we cannot chose our end
The curtain falls, dramatically
As He wishes
Almighty is yet to pronounce his pious verdict on…
Who is smarter of the two sexes?
Prayer fuels a devotee
I surmise!
Even when gods are presented with Truths
They think twice before judging!
Be afraid of Inflicting Injustices
There is no need to understand Him with your mind game
Just trust Him
Pray God that your next Rebirth
Will give you a fair complexion
Colour of skin is something
To reckon with
Make God
Your first choice
Believing is becoming empowered
Almighty ways are least understood by people who are
impatient
Every man has his share of tragedy in this life
It is God's way of putting one's life to repurpose
Don't usurp the power of Almighty by taking revenge
One is not supposed to square his own revenge
When the time is ripe your concerns will be pacified.

BEAUTY

Simplicity just beautifies
Perfection isn't beauty
Beauty is in many manifestations imperfect
Beauty is a mind game
In which your understanding and imagination intersect
Beauty is always
Laden with innocence
Beauty is a rise from proportion and order
A virtuous personality
Beautifies beauty
Beauty is distilled Peace
The premium for looking beautiful
Is draining women out
Integrity, harmony and radiance
Are the three pillars
Around which beauty hovers
Beauty is that
Which is pleasurable
If looking and perceiving anything that
Calms
It is beauty.

FAITH

Faiths today across spectrum, have become mundane
So Healing never takes place
Faith comes from the sky
So it is Pristine
Faith is Almighty's Conscience
If you trust your abilities
Faith too gives a big push
I can definitely improve upon my past
By just becoming a perpetual Faithful
Faithfuls can never see faith
They just feel the Velvet Manifestation
Faith is an Assurance we have from the other side of the
Universe
Faith needs no eyesights
Faith is sufficiently powerful to bring back your impossibles
Faith is man's Awe.

FEAR

Fear is a feeble instinct
When chased by man
It is on a retreating spree
Fear has a fugitive dimension
Fears are your inadequacies
When man is in a perpetual state of inaction he becomes
fearful
Action breeds fearlessness
Your fear has one good asset...
It kills your ego
A man with no fears
Is a flat person
With lesser feelings
And diminished emotions.

FREEDOM

In this age of free speech
People voice their concerns in murmurs
A funny dilemma!
Freedom cannot be bestowed
It can only be earned in earnest
Freedom is an urge
It fights back
We are ruled by our self inwardly
This is the essence of free will
Freedom ought to be conditioned
Yet it is nowadays sought unfettered
Freedom gives wings
To our soul
Man is born free
Yet everyone is after his freedom
Your freedom is your responsibility too.

FUTURE

The moment your present ends
You go in the Great Lap
The extension of present always stops on the threshold
Of present itself
And ends thereafter!
There is no more travelling
Future is a desert mirage
If you long for water
You will have to walk miles!
History has taught me!
That future is wrought with uncertainties
And a never-ending script of woes
Present is a great full stop
Beyond which there are Heavens
Man's life has the future of performing his last rites
A bursting bubble is definitely, what the future looks like
A man's future is there to do justice
To his
Past
And present
The moment you are dead
Future overtakes to deal with your Karmas
The day is not far off
When Learning Machines will create Futures, even multiple
ones

And we be having choices to pick out
Future never arrives
All is Present
The great dream of science
Is to recreate Man
As per his Whims
Alas
Man has the capacity
To create
Multiple Futures!
Future and Hope mount up in the same coin
The heads and tails!
A great Future necessarily
Needs an emphatic Present
Hope and Future are twilighted in the cosmos
Through the telescopes we bring our Future admit ourself
Should we not self-pity man for this jingoism?
Future will never be reclaimed by anyone
Never just never!
We create our Future to keep us alive and be working
The projection is there to stimulate and keep us
Future is a great snatcher
It rips the ground under your feet
Future cheats by never manifesting
"Your Future is your nemesis
So don't invite it"
It shocks
Gallant spirits are thrown to winds
In this new age, nobody has any Future
Everyone was made for a specific future
My future

Your future!
May not be the same
Despite us being on the same boat!
Future is deterministic
What you do today is just superfluous
Future is man's escapism
All is present
If you are not comfortable with your present
You will definitively summon your future
Future and hope amounts to the same perspective
In fact future is a bit more secular
Hope is more cardinal
God has given man hope and future
To combat His Curses!
You can only undo your Past with your integral Future.

GROWTH and CHANGE

Growth leads to change
Change exhibits growth
There is a strong interchangeability amongst
Growth is a fresh wave
Change demands your wait
It cannot be rushed into
Patience and hard working for it
Invariably precipitates change
The inevitability of change
Is all history is about
Adaptability incorporates the change ethos
So ultimately Adaptability is the key
If you are not flexible
You will negate progression
And will wither away
No one can effect change
We can go about it
It just descends
Change is always for the better
Be for it
Go for it
And be a man of switching vibes.

HISTORY

Biases are intrinsic to human nature
Indeed it is the driving force of history
Had there been no biases
History wouldn't have led with its impetus
Victory of truth over untruths
Is the recurring and paramount theme of history through
ages
Security is the most redeeming of themes
Across history and cultures
The Heroes who die unsung and undiscovered in this world
Are surprisingly not meant for this world
Their Karmas are such that they are freed from the cycles
Of birth and death
God sings their Eulogy
History is partisan
Villains is a word taken from the lexicon of history
We find Villains in history, because history is judgemental
Historians have a self-imposed duty in creating conclusions
Those who never learn the lessons of history
Are Doomed into troubled waters
Ever since the advent of ideologies
We have been demarcated and tagged…
History teaches us those who have problems embracing
change
Are thrown to the winds

History teaches us that the colour of our skin is problematic
Pray God that the colour of the skin of every human turns
colourless
History always repeats itself
Every professional course too should teach History
It teaches us how to cope with situations
History is full of references that during crisis
Leadership never performs
A historian is basically a politician
He has flavours and colours
All history is the history of
Self-aggrandizements
In our early days
We are rushed into adopting the belief system of our
guardians
Had this been not so
History would have never seen intolerance!
Historians are invariably hired by politicians
They doctor an ideological agenda
Life began with a scramble for food
In history nobody knew their fathers
Changes never last
And this gives meaning to history
Racism is the very staple of history
History tells us that the bravest who footprinted the planet
Were the greatest of visionaries.

HUMILITY

A problem shared
Is always untied
Society is wounded
We need social healers
Humility is you bowing down amidst yourself
In this age Morality
Needs no moral reckonings
My lessons from nobody to somebody
Is my way through humility!
Humility is your perspiration in gentlemanliness
One heals when one practices humility
Humility is you being available to others
Giving people space and time
Mistakes committed should be apologized first
This is the only human way
In this world
Being Humane should come
Before Humanity
Humanity encompasses Religion
Religion is not above humanity
In our Age, unknowingly human dignity is at a loss
Whether it is through globalization we have lost it?
Or through a lack of consummate leadership
Or through our mass culture?
We have to reach out for answers!

A basic human trait: most people underrate themselves
Simplicity is an ornament
To be great, one has to be simple
To err is human
Not to err is inhumane
Nurture your soul with gratifying assumptions.

KARMA

Karma is a law of retribution
Each according to his deeds
Karma unwinds your misgivings and misdeeds
Karma never hits back, it only resurrects your doings
For the rest Almighty is there!
Your destiny is not in your hands!
But your Karma is definitely there
It often mellows your harsh destiny
Man's future is created along with his birth
Nothing can we do!
Your Karma is action
It is a backlash too
Your bad Karmas
Will chase you unto Hell
Believe in soft acts
Soft behaviour
Karma will be your ally
You can't make healthy relations, even with good people
sometimes
It is all in your Karma.

KISSES

It is said, kisses were first outperformed in Heaven!
Are Almighty gift to women
Kisses are the most pious of Reckoning
That a man showers upon his better half
Kisses are meant to put two souls in commanding positions
Equally poised
Other postures are unevenly rhythmed
Kisses are ordained
The more spit you swap
The more are you turned on
Lipsticks ruin a Man chosen by Her
Lips are overburdened with nerve endings
Juxtapose yourself two some
And feel the Fallout
In kissing you become euphoric
The Bonding becomes Great
It just de-stresses you
Too many nerves ending up on your lips
Makes it a breeding ground
For joyous embracement
Kissing is seminal
It burns calories
The best workout regime
Kisses are sumptuous.

LISTENING

A good listener
Is a man of empathy
The world has very many replies
To small listening
If you are not listening to understand anything
Throw your ears away
Listening is when
Your ears bow down
You don't have to speak much
But listen amplify
For understanding anything
Politicians are worst listeners
Listening in silence is golden
People are in the habit of replying
Even before the listening is done
A valuable trait of a happy man is
That he always listens quietly
Listening is a wise man's talking
Be always perceptive to listening
It educates!
A good listener is invariably
A good orator
An argumentative man is more likely to be one
Whose capacity to listen is impaired!

LOVE

Selfdom is being myself
For the world to love you
You must first love yourself
In this world those who are never cajoled into love
Are not the Chosen one
Man shouldn't be as generous to love everyone
Love should only be showered on loved ones
There isn't anything like blanket generosity
Love is always conditional
Be pragmatic
Avoid living in a fool's paradise
Heartbeats murmur to push love
Love is a great unsettler
Despite all its virtues
Sometimes love frightens!
In any pristine love
Words are superfluous
Like faith
Love too is blind
A successful man loves himself all along
Love is a Bubble
Love is one's capacity
To dispense empathy
Inwardly, love is infused
Outwardly, it has two souls

Your love for yourself
Is the only threshold
Fall in love with your grace
How will you learn to love yourself?
What is the tricky part?
Just inject discipline in it
And you shall be taller before a mirror
Love needs no colours
It is blind.

MAN

Your Threshold ought to be your concern
Man is a one-stop remedy
And genesis for all that is Good
Your reality is
For you only
Give anyone your humility
He becomes your slave
Believing in yourself
Is the only discovery needed for!
Everyone is seen chasing
Better times
One is never in tune with the present good times
Peace inside
Tame your shouts outside
Your gut feeling is the only worthwhile alarm of your body
Good things are always on your way
For every person
Your wait is what matters
Learn the art of shrinking into yourself
Compete with your empathy full glass
Rejections in life are your steps towards
Your total integration with life
Don't unnecessarily put a brave front
Share it out
Sharing is solving
The premium on performing
The expectation from a man to perform well

Is draining out energies of even a commoner
"My greatest weakness is that I am too open
Adversaries land up at my doorsteps"
Don't try shining before the world
You age fast
If you have a Why?
Then you can manifest anything
Can put yourself under correction
When we crave for things outside our control
We forfeit our vision and clarity to be successful
A man's flexibility is the key
To his fast progress
Vibrant reflexes make him grow tall
Pushing oneself forward is the essence of life
Never inflate your hopes
Always be seized of contexts
You would reap successes
Heart is always reflected in man's action
After certain age a man doesn't need hope to live
He lives on accrued blisses
"As civilization advances
Man's capacity to respond to change diminishes
This is what we call The Law of Diminishing Returns"
Selfdom is being myself
For the world to love you
You must first love yourself
We should learn to grow together
And accompany people of all shades in our journey
Towards a destination which fulfils everyone's dream
Superiority complex is always
A trait of a sick mind
By chasing our dreams we become a habitual sprinter
A man who is seen making everybody happy
Is in fact not being true to himself

Once I shed tears caring too much about other's opinion
I become mature
I become confident
My sail is through
As we tend to extend the horizon of our mind
We tend to become more selfish
A primitive mind has more solace
Choice is one act that a man prefers to make it alone
Capitalism is becoming vibeless because
We patronized the inhumane dictum
… Do it Before you Die
Crazy mind is a fertile mind
So it is a fountainhead of shining ideas
A healthy mind is never creative
Once you are crazy, God has wished you to
Be a cut above the rest
Put hard work in anything
It will glow
Life is always unjust to those
Who are just to themselves
For a Lucky man success is a routine affair
Opportunities are missed when you are not lucky
Future is decided by the toil of your present
A mind which reacts too often is a creative mind
Nobody supports anybody
At the end of the day
You are compelled to be your own supporter
A successful person may not be valuable, sometimes
But a valuable person is always a flagbearer.

MYSELF

Your credibility is your crown
Don't just stake!
Swimming upstream is creating your person
Worry is self-destruction
Being accountable is practising transparency
Poise is inner peace
It is self-contentment
Every man has his share of attitudes
But we should beware of attitudinal trajectory
It harms
Its breeding ground is Affluence
Your positive vibes are the sole fuel for your inspirational
aura
You have to be crazy in your doings
Our instincts are blissful guides
Those follow, are always rightly placed
Tomorrow exists in the lexicon of Braves
Your greatness lies in...
To make yourself available to others
In a blink of an eye
You accessibility is what makes you
Meaningful
Don't just and never work too hard
Just do your peddling in your own way
A workaholic is no better than an alcoholic

Sometimes being blunt pays
You are seen as honest
You have the courage to put
Veracity across.

PERSISTENCE

You don't have to be an artistic genius to make your life a
Masterpiece
Simply your courage and humility presents it with a great
design
Perseverance and patience are the leaders in all
Monumental assignments
I had the strength of perseverance
Upon the idea
That I executed
If you consume perseverance
You can generate luck
You should always evoke perseverance
To stay relevant in these fast changing times
For success what clicks is
Your persistence to stay in the battlefield
Perseverance is flexibility
You just rub off storms by being flexible
Obsession with something
Is your perseverance.

SILENCE

The best apology is to be silent
Amidst controversy
Every growth needs silence
Don't compel people to listen to your silence
It's just very personal!
A man in silence is invariably fearful of a loudness
If one chooses to love anyone in silence
It becomes an unending tale of love
Shouts are insecurities
And silence is larger than your words
Silence summons strength
Silence is one of your many answers!
Silence is a slayer of man's duality
You grow by its practice
And become serene
There is a voice too in silence
Silence is always answerable to you
Silence sometimes is dumb
Silence is a joy too
Silence sees a growth in a man
Very often practice it!
In religions too
Silence is revered.

SUCCESS

Passionate and enthusiastic are the unstoppables of society
Everyone is not born to be successful
Majority of such stories are soaked in sweat
Being fearless is what connects with success
You cannot jump to successes
Small steps are always more convenient
If you are Integral
Your run is assured
Success is always pleasure wearing
Wearing your own toil and perseverance
There are people who jump failures
And land on the threshold of success
The lesson says...
Failures aren't necessary for success
Success is not something which is presented on a platter
You have to earn it all along
If you are not hungry
Success will elude you
Once you are successful
It forever becomes an addiction
Success always arrives late
At times when you are on the verge of gasping
As you climb the ladder of success
You naturally bend
Towards Mother Earth

There is nothing like riding elevators for success
For success you have to leave uncountable footprints
Success that trickles down
Is everlasting
Rejection is delayed success
A successful man has a thousand failures in his
Countdown
Success is the monopoly of hard-working people.

TRUTH

Your hidden untruth
is invariably your real truth
Truth wears a radiant face
My urge is to become truthful
Herein lies my motivation
Truth is the greatest Self…
A defender, it needs no ally
We have to see the becoming of our own truths
Nobody else will
Facing the truth is an inconvenient truth
Truth always stands bare, with no attire
It is immortal
Inner vibrations generate outer gestures—
postures of truth the body inhabits says:
Body language invariably tells the truth
As infinity's light is never compromised
Make yourself non-negotiable and, with it, your integrity
Truth becomes pervasive.

WISDOM

Don't adore yourself with success
You might not live in peace
Go for contentment
A wiser man's outlook
Letting things go is a wise predicament
It comes with age
Wisdom comes after lifelong
Encounter and your crossroads with life
After gaining wisdom one becomes a Stoic
If you have invested in Ageing
Wisdom ought to be at your doorsteps!

WOMAN

Loving a son for a mother is always more
Gratifying,
Than loving her daughter
A woman consumes half her life in hairdressing!
make-ups!
A study has come out which says
"Women always twist a given reality"
The problem with modern women is that
They aspire for beauty and youthfulness
In which there is no cut-off
The new mantra of agelessness
This creates imbalances
My mantra for women is?
Come on… Don't just fear men
Man is always awed with your innateness to fuel Creation
Husband and wife can live a blissful life
Provided there is a consensus on basic differences
The collective wisdom of women is more harnessing
Than that of men!
Women should always be complimented
For their body's grit
Never rush into a marriage
Take your time
You will not regret
Women ought to be there, everywhere

Where decision making takes place
The enigma of... Miss or Mrs
Is most sought after by men...
Women's upbringing should be such that
She only has to be wrong once
Women's acts ought to manifest virtues
It should be her living syndrome
Honouring a woman is
Accepting yourself too
Marriage is a covenant, wherein the husband is always at
loggerheads
I never felt the bond between father and daughter
Nor do I know the sublimity of a brother-sister bond
Don't be bothered
I don't have either!
My poor Misluck
Marriage is a passport for women after which she is free to
exercise her free will
A mother is a Redeemer
Par excellence
The rise of women power
Is the century's most worthwhile narrative.